The Clock That Had No Hands

Also from Westphalia Press
westphaliapress.org

The Idea of the Digital University

Dialogue in the Roman-Greco World

The History of Photography

International or Local Ownership?: Security Sector Development in Post-Independent Kosovo

Lankes, His Woodcut Bookplates

Opportunity and Horatio Alger

The Role of Theory in Policy Analysis

The Little Confectioner

Non Profit Organizations and Disaster

The Idea of Neoliberalism: The Emperor Has Threadbare Contemporary Clothes

Social Satire and the Modern Novel

Ukraine vs. Russia: Revolution, Democracy and War: Selected Articles and Blogs, 2010-2016

James Martineau and Rebuilding Theology

A Strategy for Implementing the Reconciliation Process

Issues in Maritime Cyber Security

A Different Dimension: Reflections on the History of Transpersonal Thought

Iran: Who Is Really In Charge?

Contracting, Logistics, Reverse Logistics: The Project, Program and Portfolio Approach

Unworkable Conservatism: Small Government, Freemarkets, and Impracticality

Springfield: The Novel

Lariats and Lassos

Ongoing Issues in Georgian Policy and Public Administration

Growing Inequality: Bridging Complex Systems, Population Health and Health Disparities

Designing, Adapting, Strategizing in Online Education

Pacific Hurtgen: The American Army in Northern Luzon, 1945

Natural Gas as an Instrument of Russian State Power

New Frontiers in Criminology

Feeding the Global South

Beijing Express: How to Understand New China

The Rise of the Book Plate: An Exemplative of the Art

The Clock That Had No Hands
and Nineteen Other Essays
About Advertising

by Herbert Kaufman

WESTPHALIA PRESS
An Imprint of Policy Studies Organization

The Clock That Had No Hands and Nineteen Other Essays About Advertising
All Rights Reserved © 2018 by Policy Studies Organization

Westphalia Press
An imprint of Policy Studies Organization
1527 New Hampshire Ave., NW
Washington, D.C. 20036
info@ipsonet.org

ISBN-13: 978-1-63391-640-1
ISBN-10: 1-63391-640-5

Cover design by Jeffrey Barnes:
jbarnesbook.design

Daniel Gutierrez-Sandoval, Executive Director
PSO and Westphalia Press

Updated material and comments on this edition
can be found at the Westphalia Press website:
www.westphaliapress.org

*The Clock that Had
no Hands*

The Clock that Had no Hands

And Nineteen Other Essays About Advertising

By
Herbert Kaufman

New York
George H. Doran Company

COPYRIGHT, 1908
BY THE CHICAGO TRIBUNE
COPYRIGHT, 1912
GEORGE H. DORAN COMPANY

THE·PLIMPTON·PRESS
[W·D·O]
NORWOOD·MASS·U·S·A

Contents

	PAGE
THE CLOCK THAT HAD NO HANDS . . .	1
THE CANNON THAT MODERNIZED JAPAN .	7
THE TAILOR WHO PAID TOO MUCH . . .	13
THE MAN WHO RETREATS BEFORE HIS DEFEAT	19
THE DOLLAR THAT CAN'T BE SPENT . .	25
THE PASS OF THERMOPYLAE	31
THE PERAMBULATING SHOWCASE . . .	37
HOW ALEXANDER UNTIED THE KNOT .	43
IF IT FITS YOU, WEAR THIS CAP . . .	49
YOU MUST IRRIGATE YOUR NEIGHBORHOOD	55
CATO'S FOLLOW-UP SYSTEM	61
HOW TO WRITE RETAIL ADVERTISING COPY	67
THE DIFFERENCE BETWEEN AMUSING AND CONVINCING	75
SOME DON'TS WHEN YOU DO ADVERTISE	79
THE DOCTOR WHOSE PATIENTS HANG ON .	85
THE HORSE THAT DREW THE LOAD . . .	91
THE CELLAR HOLE AND THE SEWER HOLE	97
THE NEIGHBORHOOD OF YOUR ADVERTISING	103
THE MISTAKE OF THE BIG STEAK . . .	109
THE OMELETTE SOUFFLÉ	113

The Clock that Had no Hands

The Clock that Had no Hands

NEWSPAPER advertising is to business, what hands are to a clock. It is a direct and *certain* means of letting the public know *what you are doing*. In these days of intense and vigilant commercial contest, a dealer who does not advertise is like *a clock that has no hands*. He has no way of recording his movements. He can no more expect a twentieth century success with nineteenth century methods, than he can wear the same sized shoes as a *man*, which fitted him in his *boyhood*.

His father and mother were content with neighborhood shops and bobtail cars; nothing better could be had in their day. They were accustomed to *seek* the merchant instead of being sought *by* him. They dealt "around the corner" in one-story shops

4 *The Clock that Had no Hands*

which depended upon the *immediate friends* of the dealer for support. So long as the city was made up of such neighborhood units, each with a full outfit of butchers, bakers, clothiers, jewelers, furniture dealers and shoemakers, it was possible for the proprietors of these little establishments to exist and make a profit.

But as population increased, transit facilities spread, sections became specialized, block after block was entirely devoted to stores, and mile after mile became solely occupied by homes.

The purchaser and the storekeeper *grew farther and farther apart*. It was *necessary* for the merchant to find a *substitute* for his direct personality, which *no longer served* to draw customers to his door. *He had to have a bond between the commercial center and the home center*. Rapid transit eliminated distance but advertising was necessary to inform people *where* he was located and *what he had to sell*. It was a natural outgrowth of changed conditions — the beginning of *a new era* in trade which no longer relied upon personal acquaintance for success.

The Clock that Had no Hands

Something more wonderful than the fabled philosopher's stone came into being, and the beginnings of *fortunes which would pass the hundred million mark and place tradesmen's daughters* upon *Oriental thrones* grew from this new force. Within fifty years it has become as vital to industry as *steam* to *commerce*.

Advertising is *not* a *luxury* nor a *debatable policy. It has proven its case.* Its record is traced in the skylines of cities where a hundred towering buildings stand as a lesson of reproach to the men who had the *opportunity* but *not* the *foresight*, and furnish a constant inspiration to the *young merchant* at the *threshold* of his career.

The Cannon that Modernized Japan

The Cannon that Modernized Japan

BUSINESS is no longer a man to man contact, in which the seller and the buyer establish a *personal* bond, any more than battle is a hand-to-hand grapple wherein bone and muscle and sinew decide the outcome. *Trade* as well as *war* has changed aspect — *both are now fought at long range.*

Just as a present day army of heroes would have no opportunity to display the *individual* valor of its members, just so a merchant who counts upon his direct acquaintanceship for success, is a relic of the past — *a business dodo.*

Japan changed her policy of exclusion to foreigners, after a fleet of warships battered down the Satsuma fortifications. The Samurai, who had hitherto considered their blades and bows efficient, discovered that one cannon was mightier than all the swords in creation—*if they could not get near enough to use them.* Japan profited by the lesson. She did not wait until *further* ramparts were pounded to pieces but was satisfied with her *one* experience and proceeded to modernize her methods.

The merchant who doesn't advertise is pretty much in the same position as that in which Japan stood when her eyes were opened to the fact that *times had changed.* The long range publicity of a competitor will as surely destroy his business as the cannon of the foreigners crumbled the walls of Satsuma. Unless you take the lesson to heart, unless you *realize* the importance of advertising, not only as a means of *extending* your business but for *defending* it as well, you must be prepared to face the consequences of a folly as great as that of a duelist who expects to survive in a contest in which his *adversary* bears a *sword twice the length of his own.*

Don't think that it's *too late* to begin because there are so many stores which have had the advantage of years of cumulative advertising. The city is growing. It will grow even more next year. It needs *increased trading facilities* just as it's hungry for new neighborhoods.

But it will never again support neighborhood stores. Newspaper advertising has reduced the value of being *locally prominent*, and five cent street car fares have cut out the advantage of being *"around the corner."* A store five miles away, can reach out through the columns of the daily newspaper and draw your next door neighbor to its aisles, while you sit by and see the people on your own block enticed away, without your being able to retaliate or secure *new* customers to take their place.

It is not a question of your ability to *stand the cost* of advertising but of being able to *survive without it*. The thing you have to consider is not only an *extension* of your business but of holding *what you already have*.

Advertising is an *investment*, the cost of which is in the same proportion to its *returns* as *seeds* are to the *harvest*. And it is just as preposterous for you to consider publicity as an expense, as it would be for a farmer to hesitate over purchasing a *fertilizer*, if he discovered that he could *profitably increase* his crops by *employing* it.

*The Tailor who Paid
too Much*

The Tailor who Paid too Much

I WAS buying a cigar last week when a man dropped into the shop and after making a purchase told the proprietor that he had started a clothes shop around the corner and quoted him prices, with the assurance of best garments and terms.

After he left the cigar man turned to me and said:

"Enterprising fellow, that, he'll get along."

"But he *won't*," I replied, "and, furthermore, I'll wager you that he hasn't the sort of clothes shop that will *enable* him to."

"What made you think that?" queried the man behind the counter.

"His theories are wrong," I explained; "he's relying upon word of mouth publicity to build up his business and he can't *inter-*

view enough individuals to compete with a merchant, who has sense enough to say the *same* things he told you, to a *hundred thousand* men, while he is telling it to *one*. Besides, his method of advertising is *too expensive*. Suppose he sees a *hundred* persons every day. First of all, he is robbing his business of its necessary direction and besides, he is spending too much to reach every man he solicits."

"I don't quite follow you."

"Well, as the proprietor of a clothes shop his own time is so valuable that I am very conservative in my estimate when I put the cost of his soliciting at five cents a head.

"Now, if he were *really* able and clever he would discover that he can talk to hundreds of thousands of people at a tenth of a cent per individual. There is not a newspaper in town the advertising rate of which is $1.00 per thousand circulation, for a space big enough in which to *display what he said to you*."

"I never looked at it *that* way," said the cigar man.

It's only "*the man who hasn't looked at*

Tailor who Paid too Much

it that way," who hesitates for an instant over the advisability and profitableness of newspaper publicity.

Newspaper advertising is the cheapest channel of communication ever established by man. A thousand letters with one-cent stamps, will easily cost fifteen dollars and not one envelope in ten will be opened because *the very postage* is an invitation to the wastebasket.

If there were anything *cheaper* rest assured that the greatest merchants in America would not spend individual sums ranging up to *half a million dollars a year and over*, upon this form of attracting trade.

The Man who Retreats before His Defeat

The Man who Retreats before His Defeat

ADVERTISING *isn't* magic. There is no element of the black art about it. In its best and highest form it is *plain* talk, *sane* talk — *selling* talk. Its results are in proportion to the *merit* of the subject advertised and the *ability* with which the advertising is done.

There are two great obstacles to advertising profit, and both of them arise from ignorance of the *real* functions and workings of publicity.

The first is to advertise *promises* which will not be *fulfilled*, — because all that advertising can do when it *accomplishes most*, is to influence the reader to *investigate* your claims.

If you promise the earth and deliver the moon, advertising will not pay you.

If you bring men and women to your store on *pretense* and fail to *make good*, advertising will have *harmed* you, because it has only drawn attention to the fact that you are to be *avoided*.

It is as *unjust* to charge advertising with *failure* under these conditions, as it would be for your *neighbor* to rob a bank and make you responsible for *his* misdeed. In brief, *advertised* dishonesty is *even more profitless* than *unexploited* deception.

The other great error in advertising is to expect more *out* of advertising than there is *in* it.

Advertising is seed which a merchant plants in the confidence of the community. He must allow time for it to *grow*. Every successful advertiser has to be *patient*. The time that it takes to arrive at results rests entirely with the ability and determination devoted to the work. But you cannot turn back when you have traveled half way and declare that the *path* is wrong.

You can't advertise for a *week*, and be-

The Man who Retreats 23

cause your store isn't crowded, say it hasn't *paid* you. It takes a certain period to attract the attention of readers. Everybody doesn't see what you print the *first* time it appears. More will notice your copy the *second day*, *a great many more* at the end of a month.

You cannot expect to win the confidence of the community to the same degree that other men have obtained it, without taking pretty much the same length of time that *they* did. But you *can* cut short the period between your introduction to your reader and his introduction to your *counters*, by spending *more* effort in preparing your *copy* and displaying a greater amount of convincingness.

You mustn't act like the little girl who sowed a garden and came out the *next day* expecting to find it in *full bloom*. Her father had to explain to her that plants require *roots* and that, although she could not *see* what was going on, *the seeds were doing their most important work just before the flowers showed above ground.*

So *advertising is* doing its most *important*

work before the big results eventuate, and to abandon the money which has been invested just before results arrive, is not only foolish but childish. *It would be just as logical for a farmer to desert his fields because he cannot harvest his corn a week after he planted it.*

Advertising does not require *faith* — merely *common sense*. If it is begun in doubt and relinquished before normal results can be *reasonably* looked for, the fault does not lie with the newspaper nor with publicity — the blame is solely on the head of the coward who *retreated before he was defeated*.

The Dollar that Can't be Spent

The Dollar that Can't be Spent

EVERY dollar spent in advertising is not only a *seed* dollar which *produces a profit* for the merchant, but is actually *retained* by him even *after he has paid it to the publisher.*

Advertising creates *a good will* equal to the cost of the publicity.

Advertising *really costs nothing*. While it *uses* funds it does not *use them up*. It helps the founder of a business to grow rich and then *keeps* his business alive after his death.

It eliminates the personal equation. It perpetuates confidence *in the store* and makes it possible for a merchant *to withdraw* from *business* without having the *profits* of the business *withdrawn* from *him*. It changes a *name* to an *institution* — an institution which will *survive* its builder.

28   *Dollar that Can't be Spent*

It is really an *insurance policy* which costs nothing — *pays* a premium each year instead of *calling for* one and renders it possible to change the entire personnel of a business without disturbing its prosperity.

Advertising renders the *business* stronger than the *man* — independent of his presence. It permanentizes systems of merchandising, the track of which is left for others to follow.

A business which is *not* advertised *must* rely upon the *personality* of its proprietor, and personality in business is a decreasing factor. The public *does not want to know the man* who owns the store — it isn't interested in *him* but in his goods. When an unadvertised business is sold it is only worth as much as its *stock of goods and its fixtures*. There is no good will to be paid for — *it does not exist* — it has *not* been *created*. The name over the door *means nothing* except to the limited stream of people from the immediate neighborhood, any of whom could tell you *more* about some store ten miles away which has regularly delivered its shop news to their breakfast table.

Dollar that Can't be Spent

It is as *shortsighted* for a man to build a business which *dies with his death* or ceases with his inaction, as it *is unfair* for him not to provide for the *continuance of its income to his family*.

The Pass of Thermopylae

The Pass of Thermopylae

XERXES once led a million soldiers out of Persia in an effort to capture Greece, but his invasion failed utterly, because a Spartan captain had entrenched a hundred men in a narrow mountain pass, which controlled the road into Lacedaemon. *The man who was first on the ground had the advantage.*

Advertising is full of opportunities for men who are *first* on the ground.

There are hundreds of advertising passes waiting for some one to occupy them. The first man who realizes that his line will be helped by publicity, has a *tremendous opportunity*. He can gain an advantage over his competitors that they can never possess. Those who *follow* him must spend more money to *equal* his returns. They must not only *invest as much, to get as much*, but they must as well, spend an extra sum to *counteract* the influence that he has *already established* in the community.

Whatever men sell, whether it is actual merchandise or brain vibrations, can be *more easily* sold with the aid of advertising. Not one half of the businesses which *should* be exploited are appearing in the newspapers. *Trade grows as reputation grows and advertising spreads reputation.*

If you are engaged in a line which is waiting for an advertising pioneer, realize what a wonderful chance you have of being the first of your kind to appeal directly to the public. You stand a better chance of leadership than those who have handicapped their strength, by permitting you to *get on the ground* before they could outstrip you. You gain a prestige that those who *follow* you, must spend more money to *counteract*.

If your particular line is *similar* to some other trade or business which has *already* been introduced to the reading public, it's up to you to start in *right now* and join your competitors in contesting for the attention of the community. The longer you *delay* the more you *decrease* your chances of *surviving*. Every man who outstrips you is another *opponent*, who must be met and grappled with, for *the right of way*.

The Perambulating Showcase

The Perambulating Showcase

THE newspaper is a *huge* shop window, carried about the city and delivered daily into hundreds of thousands of homes, to be examined at the leisure of the reader. This shop window is unlike the actual plate glass showcase only in *one* respect — it makes display of *descriptions* instead of *articles*.

You have often been impressed by the difference between the decorations of two window-trimmers, each of whom employed the same materials for his work. The one drew your attention and held it by the grace and cleverness and art manifested in his display. The other realized so little of the possibilities in the materials placed at his disposal, that unless some one called your attention to his mediocrities you would have gone on unconscious of their existence.

An advertiser must know that he gets his results in accordance with the *skill* exercised in preparing his verbal displays. He must make people *stop* and pause. *His copy has to stand out.*

He must not only make a show of things that are attractive to the eye but are attractive to the people's needs, as well.

The window-trimmer must not make the mistake of thinking that the showiest stocks are the most salable. The advertiser must not make the mistake of thinking that the showiest words are the most clinching.

Windows are too few in number to be used with indiscretion. The good merchant puts those goods back of his plate glass which nine people out of ten will want, once they have seen them.

The good advertiser tells about goods which nine readers out of ten will buy, if they can be convinced.

Newspaper space itself is only the window, just as the showcase is but a frame for merchandise pictures. A window on a

The Perambulating Showcase

crowded street, in the best neighborhood, where prosperous persons pass continually, is more desirable, than one in a cheap, sparsely settled neighborhood. An advertisement in a newspaper with the most readers and the most *prosperous* ones, possesses a great advantage over the same copy, in a medium circulating among persons who possess less means. It would be foolish for a shop to build its windows in an alleyway — and just as much so to put its advertising into newspapers which are distributed among "alley-dwellers."

How Alexander Untied the Knot

How Alexander Untied the Knot

ALEXANDER the Great was being shown the Gordian Knot. "It can't be untied," they told him; "every man who tried to do so, failed."

But Alexander was not discouraged because the *rest* had flunked. He simply realized that he would have to go at it in a *different* way. And instead of wasting time with his *fingers*, he drew his sword and *slashed* it apart.

Every day a great business general is shown some knot which has proven too much for his competitors, and he succeeds, because he finds a way to *cut* it. The fumbler has no show so long as there is a brother merchant who doesn't waste time trying to accomplish the impossible — who takes lessons from the *failures* about him and avoids the methods which were their downfall.

The knottiest problems in trade are:

1 — The problem of location.
2 — The problem of getting the crowds.
3 — The problem of keeping the crowds.
4 — The problem of minimizing fixed expenses.
5 — The problem of creating a valuable good will.

None of these knots is going to be untied by fumbling fingers. They are too complicated. They're all inextricably involved — so twisted and entangled that they can't be solved singly — like the Gordian knot *they must be cut through at one stroke*. And you can't cut the knot with anything but advertising — because:

1 — A store that is constantly before the people makes its own neighborhood.
2 — Crowds can be brought from anywhere by daily advertising.
3 — Customers can always be held by inducements.

How the Knot Was Untied

4 — Fixed expenses can only be reduced by increasing the volume of sales.

5 — Good will can only be created through publicity.

Advertising is breeding new giants every year and making them more powerful every hour. Publicity is the sustaining food of a *powerful* store and the only strengthening nourishment for a *weak* one. The retailer who delays his entry into advertising must pay the penalty of his procrastination by facing more giant competitors as each month of opportunity slips by.

Personal ability as a close purchaser and as a clever seller, doesn't count for a hang, so long as other men are equally well posted and wear the sword of publicity to boot. They are able to tie your business into constantly closer knots, while you cannot retaliate, because there is no knot which their advertising cannot cut for them.

Yesterday you lost a customer — today they took one — tomorrow they'll get another. You cannot cope with their competition because you haven't the weapon with which to oppose it. You can't untie your Gordian knot because it can't be *untied* — you've got to *cut* it.

You must become an advertiser or you must pay the penalty of incompetence.

You not only require the newspaper to fight for a more *hopeful tomorrow,* but to keep *today's* situation from becoming *hopeless.*

If It Fits You, Wear this Cap

If It Fits You, Wear this Cap

ADVERTISING isn't a crucible with which lazy, bigoted and incapable merchants can turn incompetency into success — but one into which brains and tenacity and courage *can* be poured and changed into dollars. It is only a short cut across the fields — *not* a moving platform. You can't "get there" without "going some."

It's a game in which the *worker* — not the *shirker* — gets rich.

By its measurement every man stands for what he *is* and for what he *does, not* for what he *was* and what he *did*.

Every day in the advertising world is *another* day and has to be taken care of with the same energy as its *yesterday*.

The quitter *can't survive* where the *plugger* has the ghost of a chance.

Advertising doesn't take the place of business talent or business management. It simply tells what a business *is* and *how* it is managed. The snob whose father *created* and who is content to live on what was *handed* to him, can't stand up against the man who knows he *must build for himself*.

What makes *you* think that *you* are entitled to prosper as well as a competitor who *works twice as hard* for his prosperity?

Why should as many people deal at *your* store, as patronize a shop that makes an endeavor to *get* their trade and shows them that it is *worth while* to come to its doors?

Why should a newspaper send as many customers to *you*, in *half* the time it took to fill an establishment which advertised *twice* as long and *paid twice as much* for its publicity?

This is the day when the *best* man wins — after he *proves* that he *is* the best man — when the *best* store wins, when it has shown that it *is* the best store — when the best *goods* win, after they've been *demonstrated to be* the best goods.

If It Fits Wear this Cap

If you want the *plum* you can't get it by lying under the *tree* with your mouth open waiting for it to drop — too many other men are willing to climb out on the limb and risk their necks in their eagerness to get it away from you.

It is a *man's* game — this advertising — just hanging on and tugging and straining all the time to *get* and *keep* ahead. It is the finite expression of the law of Competition, which sits in blind-folded justice over the markets of the world.

You Must Irrigate Your Neighborhood

You Must Irrigate Your Neighborhood

HALF a century ago there were ten million acres of land, within a thousand miles of Chicago, upon which not even a blade of grass would grow. Today upon these very deserts are wonderful orchards and tremendous wheatfields. *The soil itself was full of possibilities. What the land needed was water.* In time there came farmers who knew that they could not expect the streams *to come to them*, and so they dug ditches and *led the water to their properties* from the surrounding rivers and lakes; they tilled the earth with their *brains* as well as their *plows* — they became rich through *irrigation*.

Advertising has made thousands of men rich, just because they recognized the possibilities of utilizing the newspapers to bring streams of buyers into neighborhoods that could be made busy locations by irrigation — *by drawing people from other sections.*

The successful retailer is the man who keeps the stream of purchasers coming his way. It isn't the *spot itself* that makes the *store* pay — it's the *man* who makes the *spot* pay. Centers of trade are not selected by the public — they are created by the force which *controls* the public — the newspapers.

New neighborhoods for business are being constantly built up by men who have located themselves in streets which they have changed from deserted by-ways into teeming, jostling thoroughfares, through advertising irrigation.

The storekeeper who whines that his neighborhood holds him back is squinting at the truth — *he is hurting the neighborhood.*

If it lacks streams of buyers, he can easily enough secure them by reaching out through the columns of the daily and inducing people from *other* sections to come to him. Every time he influences a customer of a competitor he is not only irrigat-

Must Irrigate Neighborhood

ing his *own* field but is diverting the streams upon which a *non-advertising* merchant depends for existence. Men and women who live next door to a shop that does not plead for their custom will eventually be drawn to an establishment *miles* away because they have been made to believe in some advantage to be gained thereby.

The circulation of *every* daily is nothing less than a *reservoir* of buyers, from which shoppers stream in the direction that promises the *most value* for the *least money*.

The magic development of the desert lands, has its parallel in merchandising of men who consider the newspaper an irrigating power which can make *two* customers grow where *one* grew before.

About Irrigated Asparagus

Asparagus beds hold such an attraction for a man that he cannot, for some reason, depend on others to do the women's toil, they don't like to keep the beds out clean for him. Him he will eventually be drawn to cut asparagus himself. Because they have been much in debt on the asparagus, have gained the very ...

The cultivating of asparagus is nothing but a continuous spur of enjoyment which the asparagus are in the desert what grows has the most value for them in the very ...

The magic development of the desert lands has its parallel in their ambition of men who consider the newspaper an important lever which can make two spears grow where one grew before.

Cato's Follow-up System

Cato's Follow-up System

IF a man lambasted you on the eye and walked away and waited a week before he repeated the performance, he wouldn't hurt you very badly. Between attacks you would have an opportunity to recover from the effect of the first blow.

But if he smashed you and *kept mauling*, each impact of his fist would find you less able to stand the hammering, and a half-dozen jabs would probably *knock you down*.

Now advertising is, after all, a matter of *hitting the eye of the public*. If you allow too great an interval to elapse between insertions of copy the effect of the first advertisement will have worn *away* by the time you hit again. You may continue your scattered talks over a stretch of years, but you will not derive the same benefit that would result from a greater concentration. In other words, by appearing in print *every* day, you are able to get the benefit of the impression created *the day before*, and as each piece of copy makes its appearance, the result of your publicity on the reader's mind is more pronounced — you musn't stop short of a *knock-down impression*.

Persistence is the foundation of advertising success. Regularity of insertion is *just as important* as clever phrasing. The man who *hangs on* is the man who *wins out*. Cato the Elder is an example to every merchant who *uses* the newspapers and should be an inspiration to every storekeeper who does *not*. For twenty years he arose daily in the Roman senate and cried out for the destruction of Carthage. In the beginning he found his conferees very unresponsive. But he *kept on* every day, month after month and year after year, sinking into the minds of all the necessity of destroying Carthage, until he set all the senate thinking upon the subject and *in the end* Rome sent an army across the Mediterranean and ended the reign of the Hannibals and Hamilcars over northern Africa. *The persistent utterances of a single man did it.*

The history of every mercantile success is *parallel*. The advertiser who does not let a day slip by without having his say, is bound to be heard and have his influence felt. Every insertion of copy brings stronger returns, because it has the benefit of what has been said *before*, until the public's attention is like an eye that has been so repeatedly struck, that the *least touch* of suggestion will feel like a blow.

*How to Write Retail
Advertising Copy*

How to Write Retail Advertising Copy

A SKILLED layer of mosaics works with small fragments of stone — they fit into more places than the *larger* chunks.

The skilled advertiser works with small words — they fit into *more* minds than *big* phrases.

The simpler the language the greater certainty that it will be understood by the *least intelligent reader*.

The construction engineer plans his roadbed where there is a *minimum of grade* — he works along the lines of *least resistance*.

The advertisement which runs into mountainous style is badly surveyed — *all minds are not built for high grade thinking.*

Advertising must be simple. When it is tricked out with the jewelry and silks of literary expression, it looks as much out of place as *a ball dress at the breakfast table!*

The buying public is only interested in *facts*. People read advertisements to find out *what you have to sell*.

The advertiser who can fire the *most facts* in the shortest time gets the *most returns*. Blank cartridges *make noise but they do not hit* — blank talk, however clever, is only wasted space.

You force your salesmen to keep to solid facts — you don't allow *them* to sell muslin with quotations from Omar or trousers with excerpts from Marie Corelli. You must not tolerate in your *printed selling talk* anything that you are not willing to countenance in *personal salesmanship*.

Cut out clever phrases if they are inserted to the sacrifice of clear explanations — *write copy as you talk*. Only be more brief. Publicity is costlier than conversation — ranging in price downward from $10 a line; talk is not cheap but the most expensive commodity in the world.

Sketch in your ad to the stenographer. Then you will be so busy *"saying it"* that you will not have time to bother about the gewgaws of writing. Afterwards take the typewritten manuscript and cut out every word and every line that can be erased without omitting an important detail. What *remains* in the *end* is all that *really counted* in the *beginning*.

Cultivate brevity and simplicity. "Savon Français" may *look* smarter, but more people will *understand* "French Soap." Sir Isaac Newton's explanation of gravitation covers *six pages* but the schoolboy's terse and homely "What goes up must come down" clinches the whole thing in *six words*.

Indefinite talk wastes space. It is not 100% productive. The copy that omits prices sacrifices half its pulling power — it has a tendency to bring *lookers* instead of *buyers*. It often creates false impressions. Some people are bound to conceive the idea that the goods are *higher priced* than in *reality* — others, by the same token, are just as likely to infer that the prices are *lower* and go away thinking that you have exaggerated your statements.

The reader must be *searched out* by the copy. Big space is cheapest because it *doesn't waste a single eye*. Publicity must be on the *offensive*. There are far too many advertisers who keep their lights on top *of* their bushel — the average citizen *hasn't time* to overturn your bushel.

Small space is expensive. Like a *one-flake snowstorm*, there is not enough of it to lay.

Space is a *comparative matter* after all. It is not a case of *how much* is used as *how it is used*. The passengers on the limited express may realize that Jones has tacked a twelve-inch shingle on every post and fence for a stretch of five miles, but they are *going too fast* to make out what the shingles say, yet the two feet letters of Brown's big bulletin board on top of the hill leap at them before they have a chance to dodge it. And at that it doesn't cost nearly so much as the *sum total* of Jones' dinky display.

Just so advertisements attractively displayed every day or every other day for a year in one big newspaper, will find the eye of *all* readers, no matter how rapidly they may be "going" through the advertising pages and produce more results than a *dozen* piking pieces of copy scattered through *half a dozen* dailies.

The Difference between Amusing and Convincing

The Difference between Amusing and Convincing

AN advertiser must realize that there is a vast difference between *amusing* people and *convincing* them. It does not pay to be "smart" at the line rate of the average first class daily. I suppose that I could draw the attention of everybody on the street by painting half of my face red and donning a suit of motley. I might have a sincere purpose in wishing *to attract* the crowd, but I would be deluding myself if I mistook the nature of their attention.

The new advertiser is especially prone to misjudge between amusing and convincing copy. A humorous picture *may* catch the eyes of *every* reader, but it won't pay as well as an illustration of *some piece of merchandise* which will strike the eye of every *buyer.* Merchants secure varying results from the same advertising space. The publisher delivers to each *the same quality of readers*, but the advertiser who plants *flippancy* in the minds of the community won't attain the benefit that is secured by the merchant who imprints *clinching* arguments there.

Always remember that the advertising sections of newspapers are no different than farming lands. And it is as preposterous to hold the publisher responsible for the outcome of unintelligent copy as it would be unjust to blame the soil for bad seed and poor culture. *Every advertiser gets exactly the same number of readers from a publisher and the same readers* — after that it's up to him — the results fluctuate in accordance with the intelligence and the pulling power of the *copy* which is inserted.

Some Don'ts when You Do Advertise

Some Don'ts when You Do Advertise

THE *price* of the gun never hits the *bull's eye*.

And the *bang* seldom rattles the bells.

It's the *hand on the trigger* that cuts the *real* figger.

The *aim's* what amounts — *that's* what makes *record* counts —

Are *you* hitting or just *wasting* shells?

Don't forget that the man who writes your copy is the man who aims your policy.

When you stop to reflect what your *space* costs and that the wrong talk is just *noise* — *bang* without *biff* — you must see the necessity and *sanity* of putting the *right man behind the gun*.

Don't tolerate an ambition on your adman's part to indulge in a lurking desire to be a literary light.

People read his advertising to discover what your buyers have just brought from the market and what you are asking for "O. N. T." They buy the *newspaper* for information and recreation and are satisfied with the degree of poetry and persiflage dished up in its *reading* columns.

Don't exaggerate. Poetic licenses are not valid in business prose. The American people *don't* want to be humbugged and the merchant who figures upon too many fools, finds *himself* looking into a mirror, usually about a half hour after the sheriff has come to look over the premises.

Don't imitate. Advertising is a *special measure* garment. Businesses are not built in *ready-made* sizes. Copy which fits somebody else's selling plans, won't fit your store without sagging at the chest or riding up at the collar. Duplicated *argument* and duplicated *results* are not twins. Your policy of publicity must be *specially* measured from your policy of merchandising.

Don't put your advertising in charge of

an amateur. Let somebody else stand the expense of his educational blunders. Remember you are making a plea before the bar of public confidence. Your ad-writer is an advocate. *Like a bad lawyer, he can lose a good case by not making the most of the facts at hand.*

Don't get the "sales" habit. "Sales" are stimulants. When held too often their effect is *weakening.* The merchant who continually yells *"bargain"* is like the old hen who was always crying "fox." When the real article did come along, none of her chicks *believed it.*

Don't use fine print. Make it easy for the reader to find out about your business. There are ten million pairs of eyeglasses worn in America, and every owner of them buys something.

And Don't start unless you mean to stick. The patron saint of the successful advertiser *hates a quitter.*

The Doctor whose Patients Hang On

The Doctor whose Patients Hang On

OUT in China *all* things are *not* topsy turvy. *Physicians are paid for keeping people well* and when their patients fall ill, their weekly remittances are stopped. The Chinese judge a medical man not by the number of years *he* lives, but by the length of time his patrons survive.

An advertising medium must be judged in the same way. The fact that it has *age* to its credit isn't so important as the *age of its advertising patronage*. Whenever a daily continues to display the store talk of the same establishment year after year, it's a pretty sure sign that the merchant has *made money* out of that newspaper, because no publication can continue to be a losing investment to its customers over a stretch of time, without the fact being discovered. And when a newspaper is not only able to boast of an honor roll of stores that have continued to appear in its pages for a stretch of decades, but at the same time demonstrates that it carries *more* business than its competitors, it has *proven its superiority* as plainly as a mountain peak which rises above its fellows.

The combination of *stability and progress* is the strongest virtue that a newspaper can possess. *Only the fit survive* — reputation is a *difficult* thing to *get* and a harder thing to *hold* — it takes *merit* to *earn* it and *character* to *maintain* it. There is a vast difference between *fame* and *notoriety*, and just as much difference between a *famous newspaper* and a *notorious one*.

Just as a manufacturer is always eager to install his choicest stocks in a store which has earned the respect of the community, just so a retailer should be anxious to insert his name in a newspaper which has *earned the respect of its readers*. The manufacturer feels that he will receive a square deal from a store which has age to its credit. He can expect as much from a newspaper which is a credit to its age!

The newspaper which outlives the rest does so because it was *best fitted to* — it had to *earn* the confidence of its readers — and *keep it*. It had to be a *better* newspaper than any other and *better* newspapers go to the homes of *better* buyers. Every bit of its circulation has the element of *quality and staying power*. And it is the *respectable, home-loving* element of every community — not the touts and the gamblers — toward which the merchant must look for his business *vertebrae* — he cannot find buyers unless he uses the *newspaper* that enters their homes. And when *he does* enter their homes he must not confuse the sheet that comes in the back gate with the newspaper that is delivered at the front door.

The Horse that Drew the Load

The Horse that Drew the Load

A MOVING van came rolling down the street the other day with a big spirited Percheron in the center and two wretched nags on either side. The Percheron was *doing all the work,* and it seemed that he would have got along far better in single harness, than he managed with his inferior mates *retarding* his speed.

The advertiser who selects a group of newspapers usually harnesses two *lame* propositions to every *pulling* newspaper on his list, and just as the van driver probably dealt out an *equal* portion of feed to each of his animals, just so many a merchant is paying practically the same rate to a *weak* daily, that he is allowing the *sturdy profitable sheet.*

Unfortunately the accepted custom of inserting the *same* advertisement in *every* paper acts to the distinct disadvantage of the *meritorious* medium. The advertiser charges the sum total of his *expense* against the sum total of his *returns*, and thereby does *himself and the best puller an injustice*, by crediting the less productive sheets with results that they have *not* earned.

It's the *pulling power* of the newspaper as well as the horse that proves its value, and if advertisers were as level headed as they should be, they would take the trouble to put every daily in which they advertise *on trial* for at least a month and advertise a different department or article in each, carefully tabulating the returns. If this were done, fifty per cent of the advertising now carried in weaker newspapers would be withdrawn and the patronage of the stronger sheets would *advance* in that proportion.

There are newspapers in many a city that are, single handed, able to build up businesses. Their circulation is solid muscle and sinew — *all pull*. It isn't the number of copies *printed* but the number of copies that reach the hands of buyers — it isn't the number of *readers* but the number of readers with *money* to spend — it isn't the *bulk* of a circulation but the amount of the circulation which is *available* to the advertiser — it isn't *fat* but *brawn* — that tell in the long run.

There are certain earmarks that indicate these strengths and weaknesses. They are as plain to the observing eye as the signs of the woods are significant to the trapper. The *news* columns tell you what you can expect out of the *advertising* columns. A newspaper *always finds* the class of readers to which it is *edited*. When its mental tone is *low* and its moral tone is *careless* depend upon it — *the readers match the medium.*

No gun can hit a target *outside* of its range. No newspaper can aim its policy in *one* direction and score in *another*. No advertiser can find a different class of men and women than the publisher has found for himself. He is judged by the company he keeps. *If he lies down with dogs he will arise with fleas.*

The Cellar Hole and the Sewer Hole

The Cellar Hole and the Sewer Hole

A COAL cart stopped before an office building in Washington and the driver dismounted, removed the cover from a manhole, ran out his chute, and proceeded to empty the load. An old negro strolled over and stood watching him. Suddenly the black man glanced down and immediately burst into a fit of uncontrollable laughter, which continued for several minutes. The cart driver looked at him in amusement. "Say, Uncle," he asked, "do you always laugh when you see coal going into a cellar?" The negro sputtered around for a few moments and then holding his hands to his aching sides managed to say, "*No, sah, but I jest busts when I sees it goin' down a sewer.*"

Cellar Hole and Sewer Hole

The advertiser who displays lack of judgment in selecting the newspapers which carry his copy often confuses the *sewer* and the *cellar*.

All the money that is put *into* newspapers isn't taken *out* again, by any means. The fact that all dailies possess a certain physical likeness, doesn't necessarily signify a similarity in character, and it's *character* in a newspaper that brings returns. The editor who conducts a journalistic sewer, finds a *different* class of readers than the publisher who respects himself enough to respect his readers.

What goes into a newspaper largely determines the class of homes into which the newspaper goes. An irresponsible, scandal-mongering, muck-raking sheet is certainly not supported by the buying classes of people. It *may be* perused by thousands of readers, but such readers are seldom purchasers of advertised goods.

It's the clean-cut, steady, normal-minded citizens who form the bone and sinew and muscle of the community. It's the sane, self-respecting, *dependable* newspaper that

Cellar Hole and Sewer Hole

enters their homes and it's the *home* sale that indicates the strength of an advertising medium.

No clean-minded father of a family wishes to have his wife and children brought in contact with the most maudlin and banal phases of life. He defends them from the sensational editor and the unpleasant advertiser. He subscribes to *a newspaper which he does not fear to leave about the house.*

Therefore, the respectable newspaper can always be counted upon to produce more sales than one which may even own a larger *circulation* but whose distribution is in ten editions among unprofitable citizens.

You can no more expect to sell goods to people who *haven't money*, than you can hope *to pluck oysters from rose-bushes.*

It isn't the number of readers *reached*, but the number of readers whose *purses* can be reached, that constitutes the value of circulation. It's one thing to arouse *their attention*, but it's a far different thing to get *their money*. *The mind may be willing, but the pocketbook may be weak.*

If you had the choice of a thousand acres

of desert land or a hundred acres of oasis, you'd select the fertile spot, realizing that the larger tract had less value because it would be less productive.

The advertiser who really understands how he is spending his money, takes care that he is not pouring his money into *deserts and sewers.*

The Neighborhood of Your Advertising

The Neighborhood

CIRCULATION is a commodity which must be bought with the same common sense used in selecting potatoes, cloth and real estate. *It can be measured and weighed* — it is *merchandise* with a *provable* value. It varies just as much as the grocer's green stuff, the tailor's fabrics and the lots of the real estate man.

Your cook refuses to accept green and rotten tomatoes at the price of perfect ones. She does not calculate the number of vegetables that are *delivered* to her, but those that she *can use*. When your wife selects a piece of cloth she first makes sure that it will serve the purpose she has in view. When you buy a piece of property you consider *the neighborhood* as well as the *ground*. Just so when you buy *advertising* you must find out how much of the circulation you *can use*. You must judge the *neighborhoods* where your copy will be read, with the same thoughtfulness that you devoted to selecting the spot where your goods are sold.

A dealer in precious stones would be foolish to open up in a tenement district, and equally short-sighted, to tell about his jewelry in a newspaper largely distributed there. Out of ten thousand men and women who might *see* what he had to say not ten of them could *afford to buy his goods*. These ten thousand readers would be mass without muscle. He could make them *willing* to do business with him, but *their incomes wouldn't let them become customers*.

One of the greatest mistakes in publicity is *to drop your lines where the fish can't take your bait*.

Circulation is, as you see, a very interesting subject, but very few people know anything about it. It would surprise you to know that this ignorance often extends to the business offices of newspapers. I have known publishers to continually mistake

The Neighborhood 107

the *class of* their readers and have met hundreds of them who had the most fantastic ideas upon the figures of their circulation.

While I would not be so harsh as to accuse them of anything more than being *mistaken*, none the less their tendency to infect *others* with this misinformation renders it extremely advisable for *you to* become a member of the Missouri society — and "*be shown.*"

Don't rely solely on circulation statements. You don't understand the tricks in their making. Make the newspaper which carries your advertisement show you the list of its advertisers. A newspaper which prints the most advertising, month after month, year after year, is always the best medium. This is equally true in New York, Chicago, Philadelphia, Kenosha and Walla Walla.

The Mistake of the Big Steak

The Mistake of the Big Steak

WATCH out for *waste* in circulation. Find out *where* your story is going to be *read*. Don't pay for planting the seed of publicity in a spot where you are not going to *harvest* the results.

The manufacturer of soap who has his goods on sale from Oskaloosa to Timbuctoo doesn't care *how widely* a newspaper circulation is scattered. Whoever reads about his product is near to *some* store or other where it is sold — but you have just *one* store.

Buying advertising circulation is very much like ordering a steak — if the waiter brings you a porter-house twice as big as your *digestion* can handle, you've paid twice as much as the steak was worth to *you*, even if it *is* worth the price to the restaurant man.

You derive your profit not from the circulation that your *advertisement* gets, but from circulation *that gets people to buy*.

If two newspapers offer you their columns and one shows a distribution almost entirely within the city and in towns that rely upon your city for buying facilities, your business can digest all of its influence. If the other has *as much circulation*, but only *one third* of it is in *local territory*, mere bulk cannot establish its value to *you* — *it's another case of the big steak* — you pay for more than you can digest. That part of its influence which is concentrated where men and women can't get your *goods* after you get their *attention*, is *sheer waste*.

By dividing the number of copies he prints into his line rate, a publisher may fallaciously demonstrate to you that his space is sold as low as that of his stronger competitors, but if half his circulation is too *far away to bring buyers*, his real *rate* is double what it seems. He is like the butcher who weighs in all the bone and sinew and fat and charges you as much for the *waste* as he does for the *meat*.

The Omelette Soufflé

The Omelette Soufflé

THERE is a vast distinction between distribution for the sake of increasing the *circulation figures* and distribution for the sake of increasing the number of *advertising responses*.

There is a difference between a circulation which strikes the *same* reader several times in the *same* day and the circulation which does *not* repeat the individual. There is a difference between circulation which is concentrated into an area from which every reader can be expected to come to your establishment, if you can *interest* him, and a circulation that spreads over half a dozen states and shows its greatest volume in territory so far from your establishment that you can't get a buyer out of ten thousand readers.

The Omelette Soufflé

You've got to weigh and measure all these things when you weigh and measure circulation figures. It isn't the number of copies *printed*, but the number of copies *sold* — not the number of papers *distributed*, but the number of papers distributed in *responsive* territory — not the number of readers *reached*, but the number of readers who have the price to *buy* what you want to *sell* — that determine the value of circulation to *you*.

You can take a single egg and whip it into an omelette soufflé which *seems* to be a *whole plateful*, but the extra bulk is just *hot air* and *sugar* — the change in form has not increased the amount of egg *substance* and it's the *substance* in circulation, just as it is the *nutrition* in the egg, that *counts*.

www.ingramcontent.com/pod-product-compliance
Lightning Source LLC
Chambersburg PA
CBHW070614050426
42450CB00011B/3058